Animal Habitats

Arctic Habitats

Written by Noah Leatherland

KidHaven PUBLISHING

Published in 2025 by
KidHaven Publishing, an Imprint of
Greenhaven Publishing, LLC
2544 Clinton St., Buffalo, NY 14224

Written by: Noah Leatherland
Edited by: Elise Carraway
Designed by: Jasmine Pointer

All facts, statistics, web addresses and URLs in this book were verified as valid and accurate at time of writing. No responsibility for any changes to external websites or references can be accepted by either the author or publisher.

Cataloging-in-Publication Data

Names: Leatherland, Noah, 1999-.
Title: Arctic habitats / Noah Leatherland.
Description: Buffalo, NY : KidHaven Publishing, 2025. | Series: Animal habitats | Includes glossary and index.
Identifiers: ISBN 9781534548183 (pbk.) | ISBN 9781534548190 (library bound) | ISBN 9781534548206 (ebook)
Subjects: LCSH: Animals--Arctic regions--Juvenile literature. | Habitat (Ecology)--Arctic regions--Juvenile literature. | Arctic regions--Juvenile literature.
Classification: LCC QL105.L43 2025 | DDC 591.75'86--dc23

Manufactured in the United States of America

CPSIA compliance information: Batch #CSKH25
For further information contact Greenhaven Publishing LLC at 1-844-317-7404.

Photo Credits. Images are courtesy of Shutterstock.com. With thanks to Getty Images, Thinkstock Photo and iStockphoto.
Recurring – MaryDesy, Zozo Kharitonova, Sylfida, inspiring.team. Cover – Nadya_Art, Vega_7, inspiring.team, Sylfida, Professional Bat, Rolau Elena, flakes. 2–3 – Djin Polsky. 4–5 – I Wayan Sumatika, Danita Delimont. 6–7 – Ludek Krona Kroneisl, Michael Wick, Zhenyakot. 8–9 – Jim Cumming. 10–11 – Jane Rix. 12–13 – Pav-Pro Photography Ltd, WendyCotie. 14–15 – Peter Krejzl, Nick Pecker. 16–17 – Oskar Liset Pryds Hansen, CC BY 4.0 <https://creativecommons.org/licenses/by/4.0>, via Wikimedia Commons, Mike Beauregard from Nunavut, Canada, CC BY 2.0 <https://creativecommons.org/licenses/by/2.0>, via Wikimedia Commons, Net Vector. 18–19 – Jamen Percy, Galina Savina, vektorkongen. 20–21 – Michal Pesata, vladhad, Krasula. 22–23 – Ondrej Prosicky, Sergey Uryadnikov.

Contents

Words that look like this can be found in the glossary on page 24.

What Is a Habitat?

A habitat is an area where animals, plants, and other living things make their homes. A living thing can find everything it needs to survive in its habitat, such as food, water, and shelter.

animals in a jungle habitat

The Arctic

There is no land at the North Pole. It is all floating ice.

The Arctic is the area surrounding the North Pole. It is a cold environment where it is hard for plants to grow. Finding food and shelter is more difficult here than in some other habitats.

Arctic Wolf

Arctic wolves have adapted to their cold environment. They have small ears that lose less heat. Their paws have adapted so that the snow and ice does not bother them.

Arctic wolves are found in Greenland and North America.

Many types of wolves dig into the ground to make their dens. However, Arctic wolves cannot dig into the permafrost. Instead, they make their dens inside caves and other cozy spaces aboveground.

The permafrost is a thick layer of soil that is frozen all year round.

Snowy Owl

The snowy owl's feathers help it survive in the cold. Most birds have <u>bare</u> legs, but snowy owls have feathers covering their legs and feet. These feathers protect them from the cold Arctic winds.

Animals need food to stay warm and give them energy to move. To save energy, snowy owls only fly in short bursts. Flying close to the ground also helps them save energy.

Snowy owls are found all over the Arctic.

Polar Bear

Polar bears are some of the biggest <u>predators</u> in the world. However, they do not break the ice when they walk on it. They have wide paws that spread their weight across the ice.

Polar bears mostly live on the Arctic sea ice.

Polar bears eat animals that have lots of blubber. Polar bears need to eat all this blubber to build up their own fat stores. It keeps them warm.

Caribou

Caribou are sometimes called reindeer.

Caribou have hooves that change with the seasons. In summer, their hooves are soft, which is better for walking on soggy ground. In winter, the hooves become thin and hard for walking on snow and ice.

The air is very cold in the Arctic. The caribou's nose warms up the air as it breathes it in. This helps stop the caribou from getting too cold.

Caribou are mainly found in North America, Europe, and Russia.

Lemming

Lemmings are herbivores, which means that they only eat plants. In the coldest months, they have to eat a lot to survive. They have very sharp teeth and claws to eat the roots of Arctic plants.

Lemmings are found all over the Arctic.

Lemmings dig burrows in the snow. Although snow is cold, burrowing into the snow keeps the lemmings warm. It is usually warmer under the snow than it is above it.

Arctic Woolly Bear Caterpillar

Arctic woolly bear caterpillars are found in Greenland and Canada.

The Arctic woolly bear caterpillar is one of the insects that lives in the Arctic. Just like other caterpillars, they eventually turn into moths. However, the cold makes this take a long time.

Arctic winters can get so cold that the caterpillars freeze. However, chemicals inside the caterpillars stop the middle of their bodies freezing. This keeps them alive. It can take seven or more years for them to become moths!

Wolverine

Wolverines often eat animals that have already been hunted by other predators. In the Arctic, these dead animals can freeze. Wolverines have very strong, sharp teeth that help them eat frozen animals.

Wolverines have big paws. The size of their paws makes it easier for them to walk and run across the snow. This helps them chase down their prey much more quickly.

Wolverines live in many places all over the Arctic.

Ermine

Ermines can be found in lots of different places across the Arctic.

Ermines are flexible creatures. Their long, thin bodies let them crawl into small spaces. This helps them find warm spots to stay in and helps them hunt down their prey.

The ermine's coat changes color with the seasons. They look brown in the summer. Then, their coats turn white in the winter. This helps them blend in with the snow and hide from predators.

brown coat

white coat

Animal Habitats

All living things have adapted to their habitats in one way or another. Animals in the same habitats might adapt in different ways. These adaptations are needed for the animals to survive.

Every habitat is important. Each habitat is home to different types of wonderful animals that live alongside each other. These habitats should all be protected so that these beautiful creatures can live on.

Glossary

adapt to change over time to suit the environment

bare not covered

blubber a thick layer of fat under the skin of some Arctic animals, such as whales and seals

chemical matter that causes changes when mixed with other matter

den a hidden home that some wild animals live in

energy the power that makes living things able to move and live

environment part of the natural world

flexible having the ability to bend and stretch

predator an animal that hunts other animals for food

prey an animal that is hunted by other animals for food

Index